Library of Congress Cataloguing-in-Publication Data
Atchison, Steven Todd, 1971-
      Misanthropy and Henry the Cat (Poetry and Prose
      1995-2001) / by S. T. Atchison - MoodSwinger's Press
      paperback ed.
      p. cm.
      ISBN 978-1-7354482-3-7
      1. Poetry   2. Humor
      I. Title
      PS3551.T36 M57 1999

Book and cover design by S. T. Atchison, Ph.D.

MoodSwinger's
   Press

MoodSwinger's Press
High Point, NC

Misanthropy
&
Henry the Cat
(Poetry and Prose 1995-2001)

by S. T. Atchison

Introduction

Writing poetry is like scraping the litter-box—something I haven't done in a while—there are some real nuggets, as well as some meaningless, sifting scoops of emptiness. A nugget like "Chianti" won the Gwendolyn Brooks Poetry Prize. "Catholic Holiday" and "Prose-'ack" were instrumental in winning a Truman Capote Scholarship in Creative Writing. Then a few near misses like a flubbed reading of "Beautiful Woman Seen Between Wal-mart and Prison" on the Bob & Sherri Show; similarly, a reading of "Ash Wednesday" for WNCW to use, which they never did.

My undergraduate years were the best decade of my life. Yeah, the 90s. These poems start out in upstate South Carolina, take a detour through Wilmington and Charlotte, North Carolina, to eventually settle in Boone. My undergraduate work at Appalachian State University resulted in some of these pieces (created under the encouraging guidance of Professors Susan Weinberg and Lynn Doyle). Boone offered some of my happiest days: newly wed behind frost bitten windows; a close-knit group of friends that gathered for dinner and board games. These poems feel like I'm back under an electric blanket with the window cracked open, inviting in the Appalachian winter.

Brrrrrrr,
S.T.A.
August, 2020

4th Grade Twang

In fourth grade the kids made fun
of my southern drawl,
and mom made me cry at lunch;
so, she had to stop leaving notes
in my *Clash of the Titans* lunchbox.

At the table, I had to sit next to the teacher,
my last name placed me first on the list,
me and the troublemakers.
I was weird, so they let me be
with my p. b. and apple jelly sandwiches
layered with Doritos.
That sweet and salty twang
gave me personality
and crunchy happiness
that carried me through the day.

The notes were under a napkin
at the bottom of the box
next to the Capri Sun
that I would fill with air,
always squirting too much in my mouth
and down my shirt.

Mom's cursive was curly enough
to be comfortable,
always proud with Xs and Os.

I'd tear up and the teacher would feign concern.
The other boys squinted.
I would say that I caught a chip in my throat.
But, Mrs. Deal knew.
My secret was safe with her.

Through the stale tin,
peanut butter, and juice
I could still catch the scent
of mom's perfume,
as if released from the sad twist
of an Oreo.

Such distance in black and white
far removed from home
fighting back sweet and salty tears.

Lake Lure Liberty

A strange independence
taking the boat without your parents
on blustery waters.
Where we were lured in wake,

walking on water,
reeling from rope.
Bottle rocket bullets,
vapor trail hsssssssss,

peppers July's sky with pops
and red sticked shrapnel.
We tried catching each other
around spin the bottle,

and tempted fate in truths or dares.
Living forever
headlong from the top of the boat house
slicing the lake

first with fingers,
and a cold surge toward breathless,
until we found up.
That first gulp of air

made us appreciate the elements.
To risk it again,
when there were so many
footprints dripped on the dock

it was hard to make a path of your own.

Summerlong (for Ginger Morrow)

I always thought you were bossy, and didn't feel comfortable telling you so, until recently, now that we're older. It seems we find ourselves circling the same argument. You state something about a proverbial drum set I had when we were little (proverbial to me because I never remember owning such a thing). But you've beat it into me until I cover my second guesses with reminders of how you made me set up Star Wars action figures for the perfect scenario: me the dark side and you the hero. And when the story lines were ready to be played out, you went home to throw Malibu Barbie down the Wet Banana.

I'd jettison through the back wood's path on my knee-skinner-trust-rust-Huffy greeting you breathless, in that Batman shirt I'd wear summer long. Only to have you kick me out of your girls' club. Which was hard to take. Aside from you and Lori and Lisa it was just me...

I'd go whine to your mom and drink real sweet tea out of blue octagon glass. Until the "girls' club," tired of gossip, clambered to the front porch for cheerleading tryouts. Me the honorary judge. Which was never fair because you were the toss-in favorite. You were my best friend.

When everyone left we'd play rock star detectives, until I had to leave you at dusk. Go back to my household of parent and garlic bread spaghetti. Trot up the woods where night fell far earlier than the sky, shielded by the light of your warm kitchen window.

"Call me tomorrow," you'd say.   ...

On the walk home I wondered what girls talked about, entire evenings on the phone, stretched on fuzzy carpet in Downy T-shirts and summer shorts, never singing Kiss songs or drumming on forgotten skins.

Marie

I drink tea from a jar
because she taught me how to keep things simple.
Standing in her canning kitchen as I ate tater tots
with mixed ketchup and mustard,
she said the tea was best with mint and lemon
on her hot southern porch,
watching the day fade from a rocking chair.

All those days I ran from my backyard to hers;
jumping off her garage, invincible in my Batman cape,
scattering squirrels with my Batarang.
I remember the sweet twang of chow-chow
coming from her kitchen.

She never talked of lovers.
I was too young to care about such things.
But she held tight to family mementos.
Looking older as she talked about the Depression,
ice blocks for refrigeration - saw dust and cigarettes,
which relate to memories of dad smoking, and fixing things
around her house.
Both of them telling tales of history, the tolls of war,
humming Baptist hymns, swapping recipes
for chicken and dumplings,
sharing pork rinds and livers.

I'd go outside to fight off Stormtroopers
and save the Princess by the end of another heroic day.

I remember skinning my knees
and getting stung on her great oak.
How she placed wet tobacco over my wounds,
gave me a jar of tea and sat me on her front porch ...

to watch the setting sun.
To feel the hard lipped ridges of the jar, mouth to mouth.
At that moment, I witnessed the slow southern nature of
things.

Tired, she went to her molding white rocker.
Smiled while chewing a sprig of mint.

Now I find her in clinks of ice, dripping jar sweats,
the smell of limas and fresh corn with watercolored sunsets.
After my long humid days,
I take the time to remove myself back to her front porch.
I can still feel that sting.
And my stomach swims much like it did
when I smelled her fried okra.

I always ate the skins
and left the rest for the dogs.

She liked me best that way.

Grounded Attic

The only time Marie would go up
would be singing her last note.
That direction is not good for frail hips and bifocals.

Her missing steps were taken in dewy grass
past the gas tank horse,
under the clothesline,
around garden tomato vines clinging to their cages,
to the small white shack,
her grounded attic.

Open the rusted latch and crooked door
to familiar drafts tarnished from brass and moss.
Military hats and clothes in plastic
among the stale boxes of Christmas past.
Her years shelved in mason jars:
chow-chow, beans with corn,
and canned screws.

Wood planks creaked an audible map
guiding her way
to stories of family holidays,
and the little boy
who rummaged her heart.

S. T. Atchison

Wood Stove

That black iron belly
pulled my daddy's back
when he moved it into the house.

Four firm feet of cold iron
stood atop red brick and ashes
from dreams burned in the hearth of home.

Mom placed her silver kettle on top
full of water and cinnamon sticks,
piping our noses with patient reminders
of bedtime stories and cedar blankets.
The water eventually evaporated,
singeing our senses with cinders of cinnamon.

I'd lie on the ashen carpet,
licking my lips with a face full of fever.
Watching the fires die to red embers
aglow like the tail lights on Main Street
of this small Baptist town
under blankets of virgin white.

Poem for Juanita Tobin

I am held at Ransom Street
by little girl footsteps
trotting behind the ghost of Simon.
Her breath blows fade-away wishes
on yesterday's dandelions
through windows where once she gained a home.
A pump organ for a four acre lot.
Four hundred dollars built those walls
that marked the years as she stood taller.

The years turned wine into vinegar.
Soaked rags in sour pasts
to fight ailments of memory,
to resurrect family
in stanzas of
sunny groves,
and tea leaf hymns.

Books confined
like boxed ancestors
that fill the corners
with dust and chance.

I am home on Ransom Street.
I take it with me.
Though my hands may rust,
I recall the feel of front porch banisters,
leaning pines,
and splintering sunsets
that brighten my corners,
marking the walls as I grow taller.

Chianti

Jesus came to me in an Italian restaurant
with a loaf of garlic bread and a bottle of Chianti.

Sat next to me and asked if I've heard
of the second coming.

I asked him what took him so long.
He smiled offering me a loaf.
"Thanks," I said, "it keeps the vampires off of me."
"They're not really immortal," Jesus says,
"they just work third shift."
He laughed while searching the room.
I guess he was looking for fellow apostles,
or foxy waitresses who bring beer with smiles.

Am I ready for the kingdom coming?
Am I ever!
"When does the bus leave?" I ask.
"Well, I thought we'd have a little celebration.
You know, before the whole thing hits the fan."
"Yeah, I understand. One last big bang,
just like the way it all began."
Everything is so cyclical.
Women, the East.
Men and Western thought have never gotten it together.

Jesus knew what it was all about:
compassion, love, fun.
He hung out with the best and the worst of 'em.

Hey, he's talking to me right now.

Jesus asks the waitress to bring some glasses.
"You'd better make it a lot," he says.
He takes his Chianti and pours drinks for everyone.
Then shouts: "This one's on me!"

We gather around to celebrate the great and glorious
time approaching.

We all get hammered
without worry of anybody
getting nailed to anything.

Prose-'ack'

My mother reminds me of my misery.
She is a good soul.
She watches and worries
with concern for my well being.

I tell her my being is doing just fine.
But, she doesn't buy this.

Living in a small town
constrains one's spirit.
Living at home
subdues the wildebeest.

So, I keep a case of beer under my bed
and an orgy in the nightstand.

Mom thinks I should go on anti-depressants.
But, I am already:
anti-choice   anti-gov't
anti-vegetarian   anti-carnivorous
anti-war   anti-peace
anti-hermitic   anti-social
anti-euphoric   anti-doldrum

So, why should I be anti-depressed?

Mom preaches of the second coming,
losing sleep wondering if I am saved.

I save: movie tickets, concert tickets,
postcards, decrepit love letters,
bleached memories, and lint from 1984.
Why wouldn't I save my soul?

We like to sit on Wheat Mountain.
We talk about writers,
the art of living,
poetry in poverty,
smidgens of religion,
old loves, gray hairs,
inflation, bloating and menopause.

We sit
looking out over Heaven's domain.
Waiting...
for the sky to fall.

Three Poets (for Frank Roache and Tim Early)

We were three.
Pompous, proud, and pious.
We were poets.

We met down at La Zappatas, a Mexican bar,
where we read poetry over a jazz band
who thought they were the shit
playing the Star Spangled Banner in the key of F minor.

While we, the poets, worked benders with words.
Smoked clove cigarettes, drank dark Mexican beer.
All the while, thinking our women were salivating,
clawing over us,
wearing our prose on their sleeves.

When in reality,
looking over the mic-stand,
there they sat at small wooden tables
gos-sipping whiskey sours.
Ignoring our noise.
We thought we were the shit,
espousing art in the key of desperation.

Catholic Holiday

The sundial on the dash reads thirty three past three,
on a guilt trip with destiny.

A Catholic Holiday.

I've hijacked the Pope Mobile to reach the masses.

Through the megaphone
I'll read scripture in daylight savings time.
Take the rosary off of the rearview.
Give my Gentile wave.

Like an armchair prophet behind bulletproof glass.
(Who needs faith when you have bulletproof glass?)
I yield to my dogma,
drive in tongues,
and throw communion wafers to the kids.
Kiss women with flair on the backs of their hands,
like Elvis circa '76 in a white rhinestone cape.

"Uh - huh!"
All mixed up from sermons shaking me
like a leaf on a fuzzy tree.
I turtle-wax metaphysical: "Is this sacred rod solar powered?
Or will it run off of holy water?"

Let's gather for prayer.
My tank's a little empty.

Beautiful Woman Seen Between Wal-mart and Prison

Small town harlot
in torn panty hose (probably the kind from the egg)
with graceful, bruised and shapely legs
under a small vinyl skirt,
a red bra bleeding through a leopard print blouse,
chick cherry lipstick, and pink heat fingernails.
I believe I caught a hint of Aviance Nightmusk
as you pushed your cart on by
filled with discount shoes, Cheerwine, Cosmopolitan,
strawberry lip-gloss, and baby wipes.

Me: dark brooding type
with beard and sunglasses standing outside
drinking a Dr. Smooth.
I said it was a nice laxative.
You laughed and said you liked my jacket,
you love the squeak of leather,
and it's so easy to wipe things off of.
We had a small conversation about flat beds and pickup lines
as you smacked your Hubba Bubba.

Well, if you like:
A.M. radio, drinking blue ribbon beer with cough syrup,
gospel music, swingin' doors, Waffle House juke boxes,
strolls around old high schools, body hair, and
Merle Haggard,
then, I'm your midnight rodeo.

Travel is limited due to parole.
But, you can ride me anytime!

Blue Ribbon's Finest

I passed my possible future:
a sure stagger with a 24 bottle balance under each arm.

I was getting fuel of one kind
as he was getting fuel of another.

His beer-belly three cases wide
protruded from a pink sleeveless t-shirt
with the declarative slogan:
       "I've spent my whole life drinking,
       the rest I've just wasted."

He was blue ribbon's finest.
A restless speakeasy
with a bottle-cap-shave peppered
with specks of spittle and flecks of ash
from hand rolled paradise.

The mad dog didn't mince words,
he just shared a few slurs.

There's a fine line between the sobriety of reality
and the obsession for oblivion.
Small things keep you grounded.
But, small things can break you,
drive you to live in a car:
rustic '68 Plymouth.
Backseat big enough
for old news and warm bottles
in cold years.

Another Morning

I wake to mornings of lost dedication
hoping to be born again
in the bottom of a cereal box.

But every morning I find
the same plastic, cheap,
broken and damaged soul
covered with flakes.

No sugar, just flakes.

And the milk is past the date.
As usual, sour.
I never eat it seems,
I just go hungry.

So, I'll wait for tomorrow's sun,
and hope one Sunday I'll find a magic box
with the right prize inside.

Little Paper Cups

Emotions cracked and leaked all your secrets,
recorded in charts by white flanked senators
who slow the world with little paper cups.
The yellow corners can't hide you.
The lunatic lunges let up on childhood shadows.

Your hands weep for familiar things:
a cat's back, a leather chair.
Not finding comfort
knotted in starched white sheets,
nor over your body
in green-tiled showers
under one pale light
to soap and shampoo with the same materials.
No hotel towels on the rack,
no mints on the pillow.
Just someone there to watch as you shave
among wilting flowers in water jars;
long stemmed and waiting,
that make you think someone cares.
Greeting-cards stale in reminder
of what you'll face
when no one holds your hand.

If you survive this,
in time, you won't know yourself.
Looking back, far removed,
those eyes will not seem like your own.
And the words written in ill-illusioned journals -
the handwriting unfamiliar.

                                        ...

It takes time to forge a new beginning
under a sky that was falling.
To let up
and open wide.

Nell

Devotion in reds and whites
painted out of focus.

Promises in oils,
life long strokes of blurred faces,
and sunsets that never escape
white railings on southern porches
or purple mountains
that bleed into all her seasons.

S. T. Atchison

Volvo in Black

Lost my lust to a Volvo in black,
and I'm drinkin' gimp beers on Pimp Street
wasting my nicotine buzz,
killing the ash on my tongue.
Missing my love far away on a moon,
in a room, in San Salvador,
eating locusts, kissing her sweating red chested man.
Natives throw buttons at her window,
avenging me.

Heat the rat tat tat
as they skip off the stone.
The rattle of my lung.

The last ripple on the water.

I Beg You to Come Back and Be Cheerful

There's a postcard
of a black and white Ginsberg
on a Manhattan rooftop.
Skinny little poet in wrinkled oxford,
military issue glasses under a military issue haircut.

There's a watch on his arm,
which is funny to me,
because I thought he only cared about *the moment*.

I guess even Beats need to keep the time.

His hand holds to a metal railing,
supports him in his sobering stupor
above the city.
Television antennae eat the sky,
steal his stamina,
his sense of the world.

Over his left shoulder is a steeple
rising from a white walled church
arched in windows.
As poignant to him
as broken stanzas.

Cool crisp concrete,
skinny poet gargoyle.
Crying for your soul.
Crying for the world's soul.

When, Allen, you should've jumped

...

through Indian summer shade,
over hollowed houses,
misplaced dreams,
cold metal rails that kept your heart
from saying what it wanted to reveal.

Your voice echoes in the steal lumber
of 7th street madmen hanging their flowers out to dry,
sopping up America
with crumbs of reality sandwiches.

*the title of this poem belongs to Mr. Ginsberg

Drain

I don't know how to spell loofah. Evidently, my word
processor has no clue. It's underlined the word in pink
squiggly-jagged lines, like the teeth of a small animal. The
replacements offered don't come close: loaf, loafer, and love.
But I need loofah. Is it l-o-o-f-a, l-o-u-f-a, l-o-f-a? Is it an f or a
ph? When you buy one, it's not on the package; you just take
it for granted that you're buying a loofah (loofa, loufa, lofa,
loupha, loopha, loofah, loophah, whoopla).

This morning as I stood under the scorching shower-head, I
could barely hear the radio through the shampoo in my ears. I
reached for the loofah, hanging from the shower knob. We
have two: a white one and a pink one. We've had the pink one
for sometime. We've had it for so long that I'm uncertain of
its original color. The white one is mine. It's the one with
body hair. My wife is terrified of it, so she's claimed the old
pink one. I'm scared of the pink one because it's not manly
enough.

I use body wash. My wife bought the stuff. Personally, I miss
my hefty white bars of Lever 2000. I miss the way Lever's
rounded rectangular shape fit perfectly in the palm of my
hand, and how the thick white lather adhered to my skin. And
the scent, not at all "girly," like this body wash stuff. I've
communicated my feelings on this issue. She's tried to
compromise. We've gone from Oil of Olay to Liquid Lever,
which gives us over 70 washes. In her eyes this saves us
money. But I just don't get it.

There was a time when I thought marriage was a little bit of
teamwork with the rewards of a twenty-four-hour booty call.
I've been sadly disillusioned. And what I have learned is that
masculinity is the first sacrificial lamb of marriage.   ...

This isn't about the fact that I'm against change or cleanliness. It's just one of those examples of the small compromises we make, cognizant or incognizant, once we've vowed our lives to each other. For better or for worse, I'll paint her toenails, buy expensive toilet paper, and watch 90210. This is what you do when you play on a team. And quite frankly, I'd much rather spend mindless hours with my wife at Wal-mart, than mindless hours on the Playstation. Okay, sometimes I need a little of my time, but in some (most) instances my wife *is* my better half.

I respect the institution. I think it's my responsibility to enact in noble husbandry; but I can't quite view the exchanging of vows as black and white as most people. I have no desire for my wife to "honor and obey." Let me reiterate the fact that masculinity is the first sacrifice in marriage, not so much masculinity as it is pride. I'm not implying that I'm "whipped." What I want to get across is that there's no me and there's no she: it's us. We confer, confide, and trust in each other.

Just as I've come to anticipate the fate of Dylan and Kelly every Wednesday night, in turn, she's patient as I click to ESPN during the commercials. Granted she hasn't come to like Gene, Paul, Ace, and Peter as much as she likes John, Paul, Ringo and George, but she doesn't deny tapping her toes to "Detroit Rock City."

Some of you may think my ideals are a little high. I'm not a dreamer. In reality, my mate is my best friend whom I love and respect. This is why my lathering tool is a puffy spongy thing. This is why I "smell nice." This is why I try to hit the drain while peeing in the shower.

August Intends

With a pawn shop engagement
I proposed at the Parkway Vu Diner
over cowboy salt shakers on a plastic table cloth.
I remember the summer rain
slamming against the window screen
seasoning our blue plate specials.
And the tea was too sweet, so we let the sky water it down.

We wanted something different.
Back then, times were hard.
Working for a living, rarely living together.
Sharing the same bed, but dreaming different dreams.
She asked if I was happy.
That was my window of proposal.
I reached across the table, handed her the box.
Her tears came down like drops off the window pane.
A silent nod was her yes.

That moment moved so slow.

Now the years have come and gone.
I can't imagine how I lived without
the scent of her tasseled hair
running over onto my pillow.
Sleeping spoons dreaming the same dream.

Time slips.
Sometimes it doesn't take full winters for the spring to fall.
And it never takes long for the grass to grow.

Hollandaise

Her dad made the sauce from scratch,
but my cheating packets will do.
She never ate ham until she had my Benedict,
strawberries, asparagus, and roses with a ring.

Our flannel sheet rollick
kicked cats and strained poses.
But her budding frown was tight in silver
from a water-weight week.

That was her favorite breakfast
on a cold jazz Sunday.
Where bedroom window frost
concealed our thick lemon kisses
from silent trees and rusting cars.

Asparagus makes strange bathroom smells
when relieved on cold porcelain
with goose flesh shivers and arctic tiles
under our bare soles.

Shoes

I wait on the edge of the bed
to the clinks from the bathroom
of love potion bottles, fingernail polish, and Poeme perfume.

I struggle to be patient
in anticipation of a Friday night between pay weeks.
Nothing special.
Sit across a cheap dinner and look at my wife.
Who by now,
has made her blue dress decisions.

She emerges from private rituals,
toweled, perfumed, plants painted kisses on my forehead.
To comb the closet
wondering what we'll do
to entertain ourselves in the purgatory of paychecks.
Overdressing the occasion,
asking me for shoes of opinion.
I'm always indecisive when SportsCenter is on.

She'll slip into that blue dress
as I pick up her silver pumps.
We'll walk over cobblestones and railways
to dance in the last nights of an Appalachian summer.
I'll place my hand on her hip as we're guided to a table,
a low lit back corner where we'll get drunk on house wine,
and slumber home together,
watch late night cable.

Empty bottles and silver pumps on the nightstand
as we fight for sleeping rights
with neighboring college kids
and the cats.

Permanent Press

My life swings monotony
with a five o'clock six pack style.
The grind.
The wife

darning socks with Satan in the basement.
Chewing lint from the dryer catch.

We'll take naps on softener sheets.

Marriage
leaves me with
laundry and lust bunnies,
meatloaf and mortgage,
nicks and nags.

But God, damn the day
when I'm no longer aroused
from picking up panties off the floor.

Misanthropy and Henry the Cat

Sitting with women,
head to a snooze of a drunk cigar
contemplating street lamps - telephones -
beer and fiber-optics.
Drinking, undulating, d. u. I am not alone.
As the women talk.
Chain smoke gossip:
   ex-boyfriends, ex-cons,
     ex-istence...

I look beyond them,
framing the window.
The cat chases false birds,
secret silhouettes.

Pauses only to lick himself,
lucky bastard.

A couple of their bitter snickers
and I'm back to reality.
"...and the worst part of it is..." says the wife
as I reach to ash, she claims the ashtray,
"men are such..."

The cat
knocks over an empty beer bottle
causing distraction.

Amid meowls and water-pistol threats
we retreat to simpler times.

MoodSwingers

We sip conjugal cocktails
at the Lava Love Lounge
while white gold bands
slip a jazz flesh beat.

My stumbling tongue of testosterone
forfeits depth perception
on this pseudo menstrual syndrome dance floor.
Where our dance is made of steps misunderstood.

I'm clumsy when it comes to sensitivity.

Matrimonial hormones do the Rumba,
with my biorhythm in 3/4 time,
and estrogen be-bops on my pituitary.

My days, now tagged by calendar pills.
Cycle swings to late weeks when:
            I cry when the Bulls lose,
            swoon over Tom Cruise missiles,
            crave bourbon bon bons,
            retain hops,
            buy beer when it's on sale,
            and get drunk in ten minutes.

Often times we take Manhattan by storm.
We sweep and swoop
and shag all night.

I'm learning the steps
with a Gene Kelly mentality.
Tap dancing on my many colors
and singing in the rain.

Rabbit Head Repentance

The memorable conversation took place on Christmas Eve, 1987. I was spending the holiday with my mother's family; my parents were already divorced by then. The family had retired to a living room ankle deep in wrapping paper where Uncle Mark was trying to reinforce a hot political issue by citing an article he read recently. But it wasn't the heated political debate that clued me in, it was my mother's statement that made my ears perk. The discussion had turned from politics to publications, and mom made the mistake of saying that she, herself, would have no qualms with my reading this particular periodical.

I remember my hands started sweating. My heart skipped a few beats. *She doesn't care?!* I was seventeen, hormonal, and far removed from maturity. Wow, she's so hip! I thought. With all we've been through, she's really opened up. Or maybe my father's absence was the contributing factor, which influenced her decision that I turn to a men's magazine.

Either way, to me, it was set in stone. She handed down the law and it was gospel. We dropped by a mall on our journey home from Greensboro to Spartanburg. It was then I put her to the test. We entered Walden-books where the publication in question was tucked behind the counter. Red faced and trembling, I went to the clerk to ask for it. Her shocked retort was that I couldn't be old enough to make such a purchase. I gave the heave-ho of my thumb over my right shoulder and said it was okay with *her*. The salesperson gasped at mom, who nodded with approval. That night I went home with pure purchasing power. I held absolute gold in my hands, as if I had found the proverbial pubescent Holy Grail.

...

It was a simple plan. Now that I possessed one issue, I'd use the subscription card with a check to spare myself monthly embarrassment. Looking back, my mother said my late high school years were a strange time, indeed. Coming home to find comic books, candy wrappers, empty beer bottles, and Playboys scattered in my room; but she understood that I was coming of age.

Now, being a devoted subscriber for the past eleven years, you'd think I'd get a VIP card, a break on subscription rates, or invitations to parties at the mansion. Hell, Hef and I should be real close. I keep hoping that maybe on my twenty-fifth year of renewal I'll get a silk robe in the mail.

One thing that I've come to realize is as you get older you start noticing little things that once you overlooked. For instance, it wasn't until a year ago that I actually *saw* the plate of wings on a Hooter's billboard. You know, the one with the girl lying on her side. I was on the coast, stranded at a stoplight, transfixed by the advertisement. My wife punched me in the arm and at that moment I noticed the plate of steaming hot wings. It was an epiphany of sorts.

I think that once you're married you start slowing down. Your metabolism comes to a grinding halt and you gain thirty pounds. You go to bed earlier and the sex comes later. You start to drive slower. It's then that you start noticing the little things. You start to read the articles. You start seeing the plate of wings instead of the waitress.

I went through proper channels with the wife in order to keep the subscription coming. That's when the trouble started. Many months I'd come home to find my issues devoid of the black plastic wrap and the thrill was gone. So, we worked out an arrangement: I at least got the privilege of opening the black wrap and then we fight over who gets to

peep through it first. Or at the very least, we sit and hunt for
the hidden rabbit head on the cover together.

We keep it in the bathroom (we don't have kids yet). I've
noticed when friends come over, girlfriends and wives, leaf
through it more than their mates do. I try to play dumb when
the ladies talk about ridiculous poses. I know they're just
trying to fetter the fantasy. The front I've learned to keep is
to cite hot political topics instead of sighting hot pictorials.
In reality: I *do* read the articles but I also notice the dishes.

Thirty-three Cents

I entered the Post Office to drop hate mail,
bills, prophetic postcards, and bombs of poetry
in the box.

At the window table was a Greek goddess.
Legs of Elysium.
Body, round in all those places with perfection.
Hair, black and tangled,
caressed her shoulders and breasts
within a clinging white blouse.

I stood enchanted for the moment.

She slowly licked.
Savoring every millimeter
of that thirty three cent old glory.

Dropped her message in the box
and slinked away from me.

God bless America.

Another Egotistical Poem

I am guilty of doing this again,
sliding into the known pleasures
of solipsism
when all I want to do
is reassure myself,
to refill my bowl
with fresh water,
to have someone to love,
and be loved;
scratched on the back,
to not ball up myself
in thrown away stanzas.

Red Sink

You're a dramatic splash in the bathroom.
Vivid crimson that knows no sadness.
Pilate would have washed his hands here.

Many a dopey dawn have I found
lipstick novels on the mirror;
reminders of life long luck,
and not forgetting my lunch.

We've mastered the art of indoor living
in clutters around you.
We bump and grind,
grope and giggle
in mascara madness.

As Henry the Cat
drinks from your ruddy bowl,
like a sphinx
over a basin in the Nile.

Risk

I want to beat my wife and rule the world.
Everything's on the table.

Aztecs eat Conquistadors.
Alexander defeats Khan.

Afghanistan is mine.
Central America surrenders.

Yet my ego trips on the borders of Peru.

You're up.

Michelle-the-Red rolls
from Iceland to greener rushes
drubbing the black Irish with domin-a-tricks.

Suddenly, a typhoon tycoon hurls waves from the east.
Cat-zilla rises claiming armies from Japan.
I repel the beast with water cannon blasts.
A small jolt to the world.

Cold stares from "The Red."
Her Spanish inquisition
leaves me feeling a little Norse.

Save Me, Bruce Willis!

I'm walking off my steady job to freelance as a vigilante.
I hear it's a wide open market these days.
I feel an undeniable urge to shoot large, hefty firearms
and destroy those lame, one-dimensional,
viciously evil characters in my life.

I'm well on my way to impressing this
secretary at a very large pharmaceutical firm.
Extremely foxy with ulterior motives.
All I need is a low-key, relatively expensive flat
that overlooks the doom of the city.
Large windows, natural wood furniture with black leather.
A really cool stereo that'll cast a green glow
over the naked damsels
draped across my couch.
I'll peel them off when I come home
from disassembling atomic bombs in the carnival park.
All those women and children who would've lost their lives
if it weren't for my sexy eyes and three day stubble.

Now, I've caught wind of an asteroid heading for Earth
with predictable plot points.
And Planet Hollywood tumbles down
from food as pre-packaged as his latest video.
Bruce, of course, they've got him on the job.
He's got the plan, the look, the muscle, that smirk, and
striptease.

I'm married, with mortgage and car payments.
A lame job with little growth.
It's too loud here.
I'm leaving.

I think I'll grab one of those little red Baywatch swimsuits
for the wife.
David Hasselhoff might be a step lower, but I can settle.

These days we're raving and drowning.

Shakespeare Buys Me Drinks

Bill,
today's poets are vulgar.
They're full of piss and froth.
Sylvia's in a jar with urine and a crucifix
and the critics call it art.

Emily D is on Prozac.
Now more disengaged
than in her previous days.

There aren't many martyrs.
We've sacrificed morality
in media soliloquies:
fifteen minutes of sensationalized sonnets.

Bill,
where do we go?
They're turning bookstores into websites,
and bomb threats on the Globe.
Poets are hollow threats.

We're in a mid-slumber dream
peeling off the labels on our blue ribbons.

Driven to tears
and drunk at the wheel.

I'll get the next round.

A Simple Slice

I took hold of your chin
and wiped the sauce with my thumb.
Which stayed sticky sweet,
red, thick,
plunged with spice from your lower lip.

The sun warmed our beer
to amber shades
while glades of grass
whirled over crumby knees.

We walked King Street in a golden slumber.
Crashed on the couch
under a window of violet sky
with scorched skin shivers.

Nestling in your Downy breast,
the comforts of summer seep into sleepy skin,
as your chin rests on my forehead.
My garlic clove pheromones
rise from salt and peppered hair
adrift siesta sighs.

Springer Showers Bring Gennifer Flowers

Dysfunctional America in aluminum houses,
I am among your numbers on orange couches
nestled in wood paneled paradise.

I long to be larger than life
on 21 inches of television.

I have a tale to tell
of finding big, red-framed beer goggles
in my Sally Jessy Raphael Happy Meal.

Or taking a gang of
street walkin'-insomniac-strippin'-vegetarian-lesbian-vampires
to Chicago;
home of the trash show and mad cow lawsuits.
Where cold green flows into fibbing, sensationalist pockets.

Jerry, here I come!
There's capital in castration.
Transfers in transvestites.
A propaganda career in the Sun Times
as a super spy pharaoh pimp with gold fingers.
Odd jobs working her majesty's secret service.

We're outta hand when famous:
pulling fangs, throwing lettuce, snorting Vivarin, and licking
lampposts.
I feel as if I could take on the W.W.F. in my faux raccoon
pimp coat.

We're chewing on egos for gullible households.
Enacting a fairy tale for violent times.
When we should all just go to bed.

Holiday Trailer

They say wise men went looking for a king, but here, they'd find a redneck nativity under a make shift porch. Where three dumb drunks huddle over a cabbage patch Jesus, swaddled in oil rags on a Budweiser crate. The shot-out bottles of Wild Turkey in the red clay yard make crystal colored snow that shimmers from the flickering Christmas lights, hung on the tool shed with care.

And someone's burned the clutch on the woodpile pickup truck by the bright blue star in the gravel drive: a control tower for this front yard landing strip. Where up on the roof a plastic Santa sits with cigarettes and blue ribbon loot in a paper sack. Now pulled by eight reindeer because Rudolph's nose was Thanksgiving target practice for little boys in holiday camouflage with pin pulled pop guns and bellies loaded on jolly Jack. Their tree stands decked in holly, while visions of venison stewed in their heads.

A Blue Ridge Christmas with P. B. R. and glee under the tree. Bonfires burning in oil can jack o' lanterns. Pistols of wishes and bottles of whiskey shot into grim gray mornings of black cold coffee, freshly chopped wood, and the mist in your bones.

They say wise men once got around by a bright star in the East, but here, there's just a Nova on blocks.

Sky-blue Bug

Do you think God ever experienced creator's block? When you really sit down to look at it, you have to wonder. The whole book of Genesis has this "wing it" attitude. First we hear about His creating mankind in "our image." (Does this refer to the Royal We?) We read about His creating male and female, yet another account puts Adam under the knife and Eve as a spare rib. So to make up for lost time, did God cut corners?

I've been sitting here contemplating a creation story of my own, one that shall be different and invigorating. My art is looking rather bleak, rather remote, rather unoriginal. My creation story has taken a turn toward non-creation. Does this make me a nihilist?

How do I defend myself?

I need another White Russian.

While pouring the half and half, I think I've realized that the world exists between rhetorical questions. In between the answers we find ourselves. In between us, lies the exchange of commerce. Do we really connect these days?

I'm running low on Kahlúa.

I considered writing my creation story based on Mary Kay Ash. I wanted to show a world through mauve colored glasses, held in place by an Italian silk scarf with a dab of Estée Lauder SPF 15 on its nose. But the image wouldn't solidify; the character's voice never came through the doubt and static in my head.

My cat is also having a hard time concentrating lately. He's taken to knocking books from the shelf. I think he's finding himself unchallenged. For a while he found solace in magnetic poetry. His dish rests near the side of the fridge. One day I came home to find his first composition near his bowl: "Am No Fresh Fish."

My cat creates poetry yet I can't write a creation myth.

We keep his toys in a basket beside the plaid love seat. My wife thinks he'll take them out during the day if he gets bored enough. He never plays with toys specifically purchased for his enjoyment. He prefers milk bottle rings and balled up paper. Just like the way he never drinks water from his bowl, he tries to sneak laps from our glasses instead, or the red sink in the bathroom. He does watch television though. Right now my wife has put the Cat Adventure Tape in the VCR. It keeps him occupied.

Earlier, the noise of two cats fighting trailed from up the street. What followed was a horrific sound of one cat choking, if you can imagine the sound of one cat choking. This bothered the whole household made up of the wife, Henry, Claudelle, and myself. Claudelle is my wife's cat, named after Camille Claudelle, the sculptress. The other cat I named after Henry Miller.

What a nerd I can be sometimes.

This evening I've tried my usual writing tricks without the desired result. At first, things seemed as if they were working out to my inspirational advantage. All day I've had the pleasure of the cold and the rain. I've felt ecstatically mopey. I sat on our deck that overlooked the college apartments while I smoked a get-me-in-the-fucking-writing-mood cigarette. I stared at a sky blue '99 Volkswagen Bug until I felt the oncoming of a "wing it" attitude where I thought the voice of Mary Kay Ash could crystallize. Yet all I could mentally muster was the sight of the gilded gleaming sticker on the back window of her pink Cadillac.

My muse crushed under the wheel of white-walled doubt. The sky a shade of effervescent rouge.

At a Hopeful Pace

I watched the shadow of your belly
promenade the Franklin Street sidewalk
full of Echo in storefront glass.

Where mannequins' fishy, plastic eyes
frenzied full of envy,
watered for the swell of your embryonic ocean

and amniotic verse,
cool as a mandarin orange,
as green as bell pepper.

I pictured ourselves
miraged in reflection
my head to your belly,

hammer and anvil
on two separate beats.
Swim impatiently

to speak, to spin,
to catch my awkward breath,
a few strides behind.

If I had known what to say,
I would have finished
our conversation,

instead of fumbling for
wisecracks in sidewalks
or dancing with your shadow.

Move the Boundary (for Raymond Carver)

We once limited smoking to outside the house,
though I have moved the boundary
into the kitchen.
At the breakfast table
beside the back screen door,
the plumes float inevitably everywhere
leaving nicotine stains on cabinet drawers
and runners along the ceiling,
crowning the molding with residue.

I turn my back to the birds
that go mutilated in the minds
of our indoor cats.
Who, too, take their vice
of catnip and Pounce.

I turn black inside
reading the works,
craving Carver.

I've read a few gems already
about wives, cars, Bukowski, and bankruptcy,
as if reading my thoughts
already penned to paper,
expanding the borders
between screen doors and blackening lungs.

We strike birds
with the indoor mind.

To Kill a Sunrise

Thursday January 4, 1999 7:50 AM ET
Car Thieves Drink HIV-Infected Blood RIO DE JANEIRO (Reuters) - Two
members of a gang of Brazilian car thieves in Rondonia, may have drank vials
of HIV-infected blood -- thinking it was a yogurt drink -- found in a stolen car,
officials said on Wednesday.

Rondonia, salud.
I am the wheelman
whose spine is sutured
on stolen vinyl seats.

I am the ax grinder,
handling arcs on route BR-364
like meandering river veins.

I have imbibed gifts of gold,
sweltered in the folly
of bloodline chasers.
My lifeline cut short
by an inebriated deduction,
dry iced and melting
in my veins
residuum death.

These days are my last.
Rerouting the work of one man
on the untamed road toward Porto Velho.
My spine splits sanguine
spreads across a swelling horizon
where clouds stall,
to gaze through the shimmer
of my final glass.
Salud.

Old Heartbreak Top 40

Coming home to find you gone
felt like a party for one
with faded streamers on my bachelorhood
and crushed beer cans in the yard.

We once set the night to music
but the drink is gone.
My heart, a half-empty cup of desperation,
like the sharp twang
of toothpaste with an orange juice chaser.

Because our bed's devoid of feeling,
I'll park the car in the living room,
then sleep in the garage.
You found my stale stash of porno
when taking the mattress
and leaving the frame
of a house
with walls of white-washed whispers
family pictures,
solemn faded stains.

A blue light in the basement,
top 40 heartbreak swims up the hall.
It kills me softly on shagged carpet.
Undone by screwdrivers and Roberta Flack.

Standard Cable Disconnected (or observations of a living-room)

Gaslighted
venetian walls
a silhouette of claw and cat,
gentle gargoyle,
motor running evil
whiskers of want and a trashy mouth
comes off its perch
to mark its territory and imbibe my scent.

An empty bowl craters the kitchen floor
amidst the hairballed corners.

Fishy water,
dusty Pentium chip,
flea collars, and keyboards.

The consistent hypnotic hum of heat.
UV rays, ultra skylit,
electric snowballs on the corner trees
offer ornamental samplers with mood swings
slipping against cold comforts.

I don't miss the sun in seasonal depression.

I don't miss much at all.

Ghost on the Lane

Never trust a beer
bought by your wife's lover.
Send it back,
hail the waitress,
because the resin
in your throat
will cause you to choke.

Pain in a thumbcrack,
reminds me,
my wife left last night.
The lights of an unfamiliar car
hooked the gutter
at the end of our lane.

And in the residue of fingertips,
I realize that our lives are more fragile
than flimsy plastic cups.

I intended to take all the time in the world.

Now I feel forced to drop away
and not push through.
I see myself on release - a headpin
knocked from a distance.

I slide on the flats,
tripping the foul line,
notice something too late.
And at the end of this lane
a wax laden soul,
an afterlife of swirling marble
strikes clay pigeons.

Never trust a beer
bought by your wife's lover.
Tip the tables, spill the suds,
and as you watch your butts float aimlessly
in the arsenic pools
of a tin ashtray,
think of how fortunate you are
to pick up a spare.

Don't Wait on the Hearse to Take You to Church

Ichthus in a fender bender
bowed back – concave
made to look more like a shark
than the salvation of men.

In front of me,
a dent driven Cadillac
that's the color of Lazarus.
A back bumper chrome altar,
a shimmering marquee of bumperstickers
preaching cautionary reminders:
"Keep using my name in vain
and I'll make the rush hour longer."

Purgatory means waiting
under these red lights.

Was that His voice
resonating through the sockets of my skull?
Or was that the A.M.
picked up by the tin in my teeth?

Green lights on Good Fridays -
I continue to take
these turns too fast
racing ahead of my guardian angel.

You can tell I believe in God
by the way I drive.

On fumes
damned and taking a chance
that the gas light means fifteen more miles.
Praying for premonition - that blessed sight of salvation
beyond a blind man's curve.

Ash Wednesday

An old song says that Jesus wants me for a sunbeam. He can
have my low beams and my high beams because I honk for
the Lord on a stretch of Interstate 221 where God has a small
lime-green house with dark shutters. Although I've never met
him, I've seen him. I've seen him propped up in a rickety lawn
chair drinking a tall glass of lemonade. I've seen him feeding
his cat on his front porch, mowing the lawn, and putting
flowing wet white robes out to dry. I know that God exists
and he lives in North Cove, North Carolina.

There's a sign on a curb shoulder standing low and close to
the road. In big bold black letters it warns: "PREPARE TO
MEET GOD!" I find that sign very odd. Out in the middle of
nowhere, then "PREPARE TO MEET GOD!" In a biblical
font that echoes in my head; it gives me cold chills. The
message isn't the most driver friendly thing to have around.
Why not, "God bless you," doesn't that seem more
comforting on a horrible two-lane road for Christ's sake?

I've honked at the Lord for years. The honking came about
because of the sign. It was the sign in conjunction with seeing
God. I remember the first time. It was a gray autumn day. He
was cutting wood while wearing red checked flannel and a
black stocking hat. He swung his hatchet straight, dividing
the logs evenly. I honked and waved, but he carried on with
his activity oblivious to passersby. He seemed so, non-
omnipotent.

Hefner Baptist, a quaint church with high glass-bottle
windows, posted the signs along the highway. The church is a
stones throw from God's house. Every time I pass the church,
I get this image of my wife in bunny ears, shy and sexy,
presenting the entranceway to a congregation decked out in

silk robes singing Madonna's "Like A Prayer." This incredible feeling of guilt intrudes upon my daydream, so I say ten Hail Marys just to cover my ass.

It was last week when I ventured out of town on business from Boone to Atlanta. It had been quite a while since I had been through North Cove. I made ready on the horn when I noticed something wasn't right. The sign was missing. A knot formed in my stomach. The church? Surely, it's still around. I hit the bend of the curve, and as I came to the straight stretch, God's house was nothing more than a pile of cinders around a lone stone chimney. A testament that he once graced us. I wondered if all artifacts made it out. Would they find the remains of the Ark? A few slabs of Commandments?

I brought the company van to a steady twelve miles an hour. I felt slow and hollowed, like a kid who lost his lucky rabbit's foot. A page was ripped from my memory. How many times had I honked and waved in good measure to a man I never knew? And all those times he must have wondered who in the hell would be taking such pains to disturb his peace.

I took the last few drags on the cigar I was smoking, watching the holy smoke rise in such horrible heat. I thought back to the days before Easter when I attended the Ash Wednesday service. The priest put a cross on my forehead: "Remember that you come from dust. And to dust you shall return." How that made me feel cold and hopeful, like a bud opening, like a drunk with a new bottle. I tossed the cigar and leaned onto the accelerator. His remains were in my mirror. It was then that I read it: "Objects are closer than they appear." And in a strange way, I found that comforting.

Help Me Through the Night (for Russ Farmer)

At the end of the road and the last sip of sanity
somewhere between her goodbye and my hello
I found my soul over a chicken omelet.
Mother and child with melted cheese, onions, tomatoes,
and home fries with R & B veggies on a platter.

At Gladys Knight's Chicken & Waffles
everybody gets love.
There's black coffee on gold records.
Waiters jig with white table cloths,
while Pips fling eggs over e-z with a *slide* of toast.

It could've been me doin' the nitty grits
in the Jamaican heat of waffle irons and spiced tea
hemispheres.

Those diced up rhythms soothed my ailing head
into southern hazes and tall jazz men
riding that midnight train through Georgia.

My spirit, sparkled and slimy,
resurrected through the runny yolk
of a sunny-side-up Atlanta dawn.

The blues over easy.

About the Author

S. T. Atchison, PhD (1971-) is a poet and prose writer. Winner of the Gwendolyn Brooks Award for Poetry (1992), and the Truman Capote Writing Scholarship (1999) at Appalachian State University.

After sacrificing his creative writing muse upon the altar of academic discourse, he descended into the 7th circle of the McIver building and eventually took a PhD in American Literature in 2008 from UNC-Greensboro.

His work has appeared in *Errant Parent*, *Endless Simmer*, *The Journal of Postcolonial Writing*, and *The Politics of Post-911 Music* (an anthology). His editorial work on his Grandfather's memoir titled *The Unseen Hand: The Experience of a WWII POW and the Death March of 1945* was released summer, 2020.